This book is dedicated to all who find Nature not an adversary to conquer and destroy, but a storehouse of infinite knowledge and experience linking man to all things past and present. They know conserving the natural environment is essential to our future well-being.

EVERGLADES
THE STORY BEHIND THE SCENERY®

by Jack de Golia

Jack de Golia, now with the U.S. Forest Service, spent many years interpreting our national parks. Jack served in both the Shark Valley and Royal Palm districts of Everglades National Park, where he developed an abiding interest in and respect for the truly unique natural world of the Everglades.

***Everglades National Park,** in south Florida, was established in 1947 to preserve the unique flora and fauna of the Everglades.*

Front cover: Great white heron, photo by Glenn Van Nimwegen. Inside front cover: Alligator, photo by Patricia Caulfield. Page 1: Snowy egret, photo by Henry R. Fox/Animals Animals. Pages 2/3: Morning storm over the Glades, photo by Glenn Van Nimwegen.

Edited by Mary L. Van Camp. Book design by K. C. DenDooven.

Seventh Printing, 1997

*A*n endless "river of grass," blown by a wind which seems to come from out of the prehistoric past, makes its imperceptible descent to the sea, harboring and nourishing within its vast bosom an abounding variety of life. This is the Everglades — broodingly beautiful, deceptively serene — a fragile world where life is held in delicate abeyance between man and nature.

A few minutes from the restless metropolis of downtown Miami lies a vast stretch of primeval quiet—a wilderness that is unique on the North American continent. It is a region about which we understand little, but we call it the *Everglades*, a name that may have a certain romantic quality but does little to convey its special character.

Thanks to a popular mythology that has grown up about the Everglades, its mention will likely conjure up an image of a quicksand-filled swamp teeming with man-eating alligators, slithering snakes, steamy, vine-choked jungles, and hordes of disease-carrying insects—all in all, a worthless, impenetrable, uncomfortable place.

The reality is of course far different. The Everglades encompasses a region so extensive and so varied that its essence cannot be captured in a single, sweeping statement. It is the shallow, pale-blue waters of Florida Bay; it is dense trees along narrow coastal creeks; it is a flowing expanse of "grass" that resembles nothing so much as a vast African savanna; it is pines and mangroves and shelly beaches and, yes, the classic, exotic swamp. It is all these things and more.

But it is the overpowering flatness of the Everglades that is its greatest impact on first sight—that, and its life, spectacular and seasonally abundant but also elusive, mysterious, and much of it microscopic! And it is precisely this landscape and the life it nourishes that make the Everglades so precious. Life here is a complex web, spun ever so delicately and attuned ever so finely to the primal elements and forces of the earth.

At the hub of this web, man, scarcely a part of the scene a century ago, has placed himself. For him the Everglades has come to mean more land on which to build cities, a source for fresh drinking water, and a place for physical and spiritual renewal. He is the one animal living here who is capable of both causing cataclysmic change and exercising careful guardianship of the status quo.

And he is the one animal living here who can appreciate all the beauty and uniqueness that the Everglades holds. Lying as it does at the edge of an urban, complex world, the region offers a tremendous opportunity for exploration and study of a world that is equally as complex. For the Everglades, despite man's encroachment, remains an original on the face of the earth, a place we are only just beginning to understand.

GLENN VAN NIMWEGEN

The Everglades is a low place in a low land. The highest point in the entire state of Florida, in its northern panhandle, is only 345 feet above sea level. But even that seems high when compared to the "Glades," as Floridians call the area that runs a hundred miles from Lake Okeechobee to Florida Bay at the southern tip of the state. The 1.5 million acres of Everglades National Park, covering about a seventh of the Everglades at its southernmost end, ranges from sea level to a "towering" twenty

The Primal Elements

feet on an Indian-made mound near Chokoloskee.

Several times in the past million years or so, the Florida peninsula has been submerged in and then resurrected from the sea, conditions caused not by land shifts but by the great continental glaciers which spread from the poles toward the equator and then in alternating periods of warm climate receded, shrinking back toward the poles. The glaciers themselves never reached this far south, but in their advance they drove before them an interesting variety of prehistoric animals—including mammoth, wolf, camel, bison, bear, saber-toothed tiger, and others who lived at one time or another in this region. While the glaciers were active, the huge amounts of water they entrapped left the Florida peninsula high and dry, but during the interglacial periods, shallow tropical seas covered the land, a result of the melting water that flowed from retreating sheets of ice.

The floor of the Everglades is rock hard but porous as a sponge. The limestone bedrock in the fresh-water Glades, with its thin covering of organic soil, is several inches underwater in the summer, but by spring the jagged pinnacles of etched, eroded limestone stand dry and white under the hot sun.

A variety of rock formations was left behind from these periods between ice ages when water covered the land. The upper Florida keys (*key* is from the Spanish *cayo,* meaning *island*) are fossil-coral reefs, similar when living to the reefs found today in the Atlantic waters of Biscayne National Park and John D. Pennekamp Coral Reef State Park. Beneath Lake Okeechobee and the northern Everglades, the rock is limestone, made up of alternating beds of hardened sea bottom (shelly, limy muds and sands) and fresh-water peat and mud. This rock layer, about a hundred thousand years old, is called the *Fort Thompson* formation. It extends south, dipping under another limestock layer of similar age, the *Miami* formation, which underlies Everglades National Park.

A digression to the Bahamas may simplify the explanation of the origin of the Miami formation: The Great Bahama Bank is submerged in a shallow, warm sea—just as Florida was when the oceans were higher. Today, as in the past, there are limestone-producing plants and animals in this sea. As the Gulf Stream sweeps by the Bahamas, it is continuously piling up a low ridge of limestone grains, in much the same manner that wind piles sand in a long dune. The limestone grains are called *oolites,* since under close examination they resemble tiny eggs (*oo* is the Latin prefix for *egg*). They are formed by the accumulation of calcium carbonate (limestone) around tiny grains of sand.

Behind the loosely piled ridge of oolites, in waters sheltered from the Gulf Stream by the ridge, are bryozoans—tiny, marine invertebrates that build branching, rock-like colonies. Unlike coral they do not build reefs, but like coral they leave their life's work behind when they die. Countless chunks of bryozoan colonies are present in the limy mud of the sea bottom.

Back in southern Florida we can see what is probably in store for the Bahamian oolitic ridge and its deposits of bryozoan colonies. About a hundred thousand years ago, when the Florida peninsula began to be exposed above sea level, the oolitic ridge on the eastern coast was washed by fresh rainwater, which dissolved some of the calcareous grains. As the rainwater evaporated, it deposited limestone in the spaces between the oolites, cementing them together and fusing them to the land below. The resulting ridge of solid rock, now called the Atlantic Coastal Ridge, extends from near Fort Lauderdale to Long Pine Key in Everglades National Park. The ridge forms one edge of the Everglades and its higher elevation provides dry land favorable to the growth of slash pine, hardwood trees—and cities.

Behind the oolitic ridge, to the west (a mirror of the way these features are aligned in the Bahamas), the bryozoan remains mixed in the sea

From the air the hammocks of the southern Everglades seem like verdant ships ploughing through the saw-grass river. From the ground each hammock has a distinctive profile, enabling trained eyes to use them as landmarks in the otherwise flat expanse of saw grass. The mounds of dry land support a variety of tropical and temperate life in combinations unique to each.

bottom were likewise exposed to air as the sea lowered. The sediment hardened into a solid but porous limestone bedrock—a vast basin featuring occasional small fossilized bryozoan shell clumps. Here and there low mounds protruded in the bedrock, extra-hard irregularities of the former sea bottom that stayed a few feet higher than the surrounding level and ranged in size from a few square feet to a few hundred acres. Today the mounds are called *hammocks*, and hardwood trees now populate these islands of high, dry ground that stand like verdant ships in the expanse of the saw-grass marsh.

The oldest rock in southern Florida is that which underlies Big Cypress Swamp. It is a limestone about six million years old—the *Tamiami* formation—composed of deposits of shelly, limy muds, and quartz sand. It is more acidic, harder, and less permeable than the Miami or Fort Thompson formations and it lies very deep under Dade County. There the Tamiami limestone underlies both the Fort Thompson and Miami formations and acts as an impervious barrier to the flow of underground water. Since the Miami and especially the Fort Thompson limestones are quite porous, acting almost as rock "sponges," the underground water reservoir thus formed is able to supply the counties of Dade, Broward, Monroe, and Palm Beach with all their fresh-water needs. This reservoir, the Biscayne Aquifer, is maintained by rainwater falling on the Glades.

The fresh water flows upon the surface of the Everglades southwesterly toward the Gulf of Mexico, but it is also flowing in an easterly direction to the Atlantic Ocean underground through the porous limestone. Because of the pressure of the fresh-water flow, sea water is prevented from intruding into the rock. Without the Everglades, then, underground sources would be contaminated by salt, and the cities of southeastern Florida would have to depend entirely upon captured rainfall for their fresh-water needs.

This watery land, the Everglades, has a solid-rock bottom. There is *no* quicksand here! Places do exist where there are deep holes in the bedrock. In other places, *marl* (limy, organic mud) or peat (resulting from years and years of rotting saw grass) lie in deep deposits on top of the limestone bedrock, disguising its presence. No wonder that those attempting to walk in Florida Bay, for instance, or along creeks in the mangroves, don't make good witnesses for the presence of bedrock! But in the fresh-water interior of the Glades, the bedrock is often visible. It juts up in some places or lurks just below the thin soil. In the pinelands the rock is eroded into miniature badlands, called "pinnacle rock." It isn't surprising that with such a varied footing, hikers often find the going slow and tricky over the rock bottom of the Everglades.

PATRICIA CAULFIELD

THE SEASONS

The climate of the area known as South Florida to its inhabitants is much like a tropical island, extending as it does so close to the tropics and surrounded as it is on three sides by warm seas. The result is a warm, aquatic land in which a multitude of plants and animals thrive.

But all is not paradise here. Each year there comes a time when the rains cease and the land may become parched and dry, when all life frantically seeks the small pools of life-giving moisture which may mean survival. It can be a matter of "feast or famine," for there are only two seasons in this land—wet and dry—and each can be extreme.

The rainy season begins in late May or June, as it does all across the Caribbean, and in the ensuing months, eighty percent of the yearly precipitation may fall. Urban residents of South Florida retreat to air-conditioned rooms as the thermometer moves sluggishly from the eighties at night to the nineties during the day and back again. Frequent afternoon thundershowers bring welcome relief from the high humidity.

In the Everglades, torrents of water rake the land in late-summer afternoons, falling with drumlike intensity from the bulbous, white thunderclouds rolling in from the Gulf of Mexico. By the end of the season, water covers the saw-grass and rush prairies. Only the hardwood hammocks in the midst of the Everglades and the high, pine- and hardwood-covered Atlantic Coastal Ridge are above water. This is the time when mosquitoes are their most visible and vexatious—the supreme example of life's exuberance. They can make summertime activities "challenging," to say the least!

The wet season is hurricane season. Florida has more hurricanes than any part of the United States. Over the nineteenth century, hurricanes have hit southern Florida at least fifty times.

Unlike many of Florida's newer (human) population, the residents of the Everglades have adapted to these great storms. Many of the tropical plants and some of the smaller animals—such as the liguus tree snail—may owe their very existence in Florida to the fact that they were transported here by hurricane winds or tides. During a storm, when winds exceed seventy-five miles per hour (some have been recorded at velocities approaching 200 miles per hour!), plant seeds are spread far and wide. And after the calm eye of a hurricane has passed, the winds begin anew and just as violently—but this time from the opposite direction.

This circular wind pattern makes hurricanes very thorough mixers, to put it mildly. In Florida Bay, where shallow water is frequently blown right out of parts of the bay by *normal* winds, hurricanes often "turn the bay upside down." The salty bay is flushed with fresh water from the hurricane's rains, and the bottom sediment is stirred and churned into the water, changing the nutrient supply of the water (and thus the balance of life) for years to come. Along the mangrove-covered coast, even very old, large trees don't escape the ravages of wind and tides gone wild. Hurricane Andrew, for instance, knocked down 70,000 acres of mangrove forest in 1992.

The day after a hurricane, when havoc is everywhere, it seems the storm was nothing but an exercise in brute destruction. Viewed from the perspective of centuries of such activity, however, it is evident that hurricanes actually provide opportunities for living things to increase—by opening up new places for sun-loving plants; by churning nutrients from marine bottoms to make them available to the pink shrimp, fish, crabs, and lobsters in the waters above; and by carrying plants and animals to new habitations.

A forest of mangroves laid to waste demonstrates the force and destruction of hurricanes. In time a new forest will emerge, recycling the material of the old.

JAMES A. KERN

The official close of hurricane season coincides with the gradual end of the rainy season in late November. From then until the following summer, in most years, very little rain falls anywhere in southern Florida, and the land gradually dries down until there is little or no surface water left. The Everglades lies in the latitude of some of the world's great deserts, a latitude of seasonal rainfall and drought. Were it not for the vast, flooded marsh and the ability of its soils to absorb and release water slowly, there would be no array of water-dependent life here. Still, the dry season challenges the survival capabilities of even the hardiest of the life found in the Everglades.

Rainfall is highly variable from year to year. While evaporation may sometimes exceed the average annual rainfall of sixty inches, as little as thirty or as much as a hundred inches of rain can fall in a particular year. Thus the dry season can be a time of extreme drought or mild drought, depending on the rainfall the previous wet season. Also, during the dry, winter season, cold fronts from the north may bring occasional frosts which prune back some of the tropical plant life and limit its northern reach.

Mammals living close to the equator tend to be smaller than their northern counterparts. The weight of this Everglades white-tail buck, for instance, may be 150 pounds, about half that of a Michigan white-tail.

The tropical zebra butterfly

By late spring or early summer, the clouds of vapor that have been accumulating in the sky above release their burdens and the rainy season is once again upon the Everglades, completing the annual cycle of flood and drought and flood.

Thus it is that the two Everglades seasons—one warm and wet, enabling life to flourish, the other dry and sometimes cold, limiting and reducing life—have made for a unique mixture of living things in the Everglades. The fact that subtropical Florida is connected to the body of the North American continent enables temperate plants and land mammals to come into the Everglades and live as neighbors to species from tropical climes. And so we may find a white-tailed deer, smaller but otherwise similar to its Michigan cousins, feeding on saw grass and walking over marine-produced limestone rock, through water brought by clouds from the warm Gulf Stream. As the deer nears a hammock—an island where the temperate, sturdy live oak may grow next to the tropical, copper-colored gumbo limbo—a zebra butterfly may flit by, much like others of its kind found farther south in the tropics of Central America.

Such a scene could occur nowhere else on the North American continent. It is unique to the Everglades, itself a unique combination of the primal elements—rock, wind, water, frost, and sun.

SUGGESTED READING

CARR, ARCHIE. *The Everglades.* New York: Time-Life Books, 1973.

CAULFIELD, PATRICIA. *Everglades.* San Francisco: Sierra Club, 1970.

DOUGLAS, MARJORIE STONEMAN. *The Everglades—River of Grass.* New York: Rinehart & Co., 1947.

HOFFMEISTER, JOHN EDWARD. *Land from the Sea: The Geologic Story of South Florida.* Coral Gables: Univ. of Miami Press, 1974.

ROBERTSON, WILLIAM B. JR. *Everglades: The Park Story.* Homestead, FL: Florida National Parks and Monuments Association, 1989.

GLENN VAN NIMWEGEN

Life in the Everglades

At first glance, the Everglades may seem nothing more than a confusing array of trees, grasslands, alligators, birds, plants, and insects in a monotonously flat landscape. But look again! There is an abundance of life here that is every bit as spectacular (and, it might be argued, immensely more rewarding) than any grand mountain vista. It is a place where tropical and temperate flora and fauna exist side by side in their natural, wild condition and pursue ages-old habits that range from commonplace to quaint to downright perplexing! And all this wealth lies in a subtropical wilderness but a short distance from one of the great metropolitan areas of the country!

The heart of this unusual land, the Everglades, is the great "river of grass," the largest saw-grass marsh in the world, a hundred miles of gently flowing water that varies up to about fifty miles in width and harbors a vast community of living things. It begins with the giant (700-square-mile) Lake Okeechobee—next to Lake Michigan the largest fresh-water lake within the Lower 48 states—which is fed by the waters of the Kissimmee Valley and a chain of lakes yet farther north. The whole region is a shallow decline that slopes southward at an average of only two inches per mile from the lake to the Gulf of Mexico.

But southern Florida is so flat that elevation changes of even a few feet may mean the difference between flooding and staying dry. And so, in the midst of the Glades, we find hammocks standing two or three feet higher than their surroundings and crowned by tropical hardwood trees which conceal the deer, raccoons, bobcats, and marsh rabbits that make these islands their homes. Here and there, scattered about the Glades, are the slightly deeper areas—ponds, sloughs (pronounced *slews*), and "gator holes," named in honor of their creator, the Glades' foremost resident, the American alligator. Here, too, the anhinga (snakebird or water turkey) dives underwater to spear fish with his sharp bill amidst a variety of birds, insects, and plants, all at home in this fresh-water habitat.

Rimming the glades community to the east, on the Atlantic Coastal Ridge, are the rocky pinelands, intermixed with hammocks similar to those found in the Glades. Here wildflowers, woodpeckers, pine warblers, raccoons, and red-shouldered hawks make up a diverse but wholly compatible community.

The temperate raccoon in a tropical scene

BRECK P. KENT/ANIMALS ANIMALS

The anhinga makes its living underwater, first spearing a fish with its razor-sharp bill, then shaking it off and flipping it into the open mouth. After a meal of fish the anhinga must spend time spreading its wings in the sun to dry and to let the sunshine reheat the water-cooled blood racing through the thin wings. This coy lady of the swamps is a graceful study in concentration as she attends to her feathers.

An eastern meadowlark sings his bright song.

GLENN VAN NIMWEGEN

The Glades is a mosaic of stands of saw grass and various rushes. Unlike the sharp-edged saw grass, rushes (above) are round and smooth, often growing in shallower water and in thinner soil. Rarely do rushes stand higher than four feet, while saw grass can form dense barriers twelve feet high.

In the transition zone, where fresh water gradually mingles with the saltwater sea, the wilderness of mangroves grows close along the creeks and sometimes over the narrow waterways. Here saltwater mosquitoes, more persistent than their fresh-water counterparts, test one's mettle. Tarpon, which reach great size, and the bottle-nosed dolphin arouse curiosity. The rare American crocodile pursues an existence whose future has been made uncertain by the destruction of its habitat. And the astonishing mammal, the plump manatee (sea cow), grazes quietly in the warm, salty water.

On the shelly beaches of storm-created Cape

A young gator and an ancient gaze

Sable, southernmost tip of the continental United States, sea turtles come ashore to lay eggs, and coastal prairies of low-growing succulents and cacti struggle for life in the salty soil. And in shallow Florida Bay, dotted by small islands, a marine world of turtle-grass flats and shelled invertebrates supports—together with the nutrient-rich mangrove estuary—a bountiful sport fishery.

These are the amazing, extensive, and diverse life communities that make up the Everglades. Together they form a complex system of cause and effect, life and death. And all are one in their dependence upon water, the life-giving "blood" of this planet.

The River

There was a time, not so long ago—in fact it was about the turn of the century—when the huge lake Okeechobee (*Oh-geh-CHOH-beh*) was not confined, and the Everglades was a pristine wilderness, by almost anybody's standards. Man was there, but his impact was so slight as to be practically non-existent.

The seasons came and the seasons went. Every summer the rains fell, and in some very wet years Okeechobee swelled and spilled its waters over the low southern lip of its saucer-like basin into a river. But Okeechobee's river was different; whereas most rivers are narrow and deep, this

Lounging is what an alligator does best. This may seem a lazy way to spend the time, but this cold-blooded reptile needs the sun to warm its body in order to function. Besides, its lethargy is deceiving—an alligator can strike like lightning! In sudden scurries and lunges, it can overpower almost any visitor to its waterhole, animals which would seem to be much quicker and capable of easily eluding the huge gator.

An alligator's engineering work—a gator hole—provides food for many other animals during the dry season. Routing out mud and plants, the alligator creates a pond to which all water-loving creatures flock, from microbes to fish and mammals. These wood storks may carry their catches as far as seventy-five miles to their young waiting on nests. Thus it is that another generation may owe its life to that ancient monarch, the alligator.

ZIG LESZCZYNSKI/ANIMALS ANIMALS

one covered more than 8 million acres; it was miles and miles wide and only one or two feet deep. Yet it *was* a river, and it flowed from the lake to the sea, albeit at a very slow rate (a quarter of a mile per day).

The Indians who lived in the river called it Pa-hay-okee (pah-HIGH-og-geh), "the grassy waters." Others, perhaps English explorers, remembering the wide, green, open spaces—the glades—of their native land, called it the "Everglades," since it seemed to stretch on forever.

During the winter, the sky was clear and the sun shone bright and hot. The river dried completely in some years and in others not much at all. In very dry years the alligator used his broad snout and powerful tail to root out mud and plants from depressions in the bedrock, wallowing and thrashing until he had reached water, thus creating the "gator holes," to which all other living things in the river flocked for water.

If there was one animal in the river who could be called the "king of beasts," it was the alligator, for he was a provider as well as a consumer of life in the Glades. Although the female alligator vigilantly guarded the nests, they were often raided by egg-hungry raccoons. Young hatching gators became food for great blue herons and sometimes

other gators, but by the time they reached several feet in length their lives could be taken only by larger gators or by men. The alligator itself ate just about every other animal found in the river, but it ate rarely, sometimes only once or twice a week. The rest of the time this descendant of the dinosaurs spent its days basking in the warm sun or lingering the in watery mud caves behind the gator holes.

During the high water of summer, the fish of

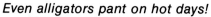
Even alligators pant on hot days!

PATRICIA CAULFIELD

17

the river thrived on the bloom of microscopic life and insect life that in turn thrived on the algae and plankton in the rising waters. Some of the algae grew in mats, called *periphyton,* which held hundreds of tiny animals. Periphyton, the bottom of the food chain, was fed on by tiny fish which were in turn preyed upon by larger fish—bream, garfish, and large-mouthed bass. The fish spread as far and as wide as the waters.

During the dry season, the water evaporated from the vast marsh and flowed off the land into the mangrove estuary and the sea. The mats of periphyton settled onto the now-dry floor of the Glades; their spongy quality protected many of the smaller creatures and their eggs from the annual winter drought. The land dried and cracked. The smell of dead fish filled the air. By late spring it seemed that only the turkey vulture and the black vulture were visible, flourishing on the death that lay all around.

But before the river dried completely, the fish and other aquatic life gathered in watery refuges where water was still to be found—the shrinking ponds and gator holes. Where in the summer the fish of the river had been spread to the horizon, now the waters of the gator holes were all that lay between them and death, and they were jammed with life. From these ponds deer drank and river otter sought fish and crayfish. The great blue, little blue, tricolored, and green-backed herons, and the snowy and great egrets gathered too and ate their fill of fish. Then these and other wading birds—the ibis, storks, and spoonbills—carried the bounty back to their young in nests within the large rookeries found throughout the region, especially in the mangroves. And so it was, not so long ago.

Today this cycle of wet and dry, of life blooming and spreading thin and then concentrating beyond belief continues, but with some changes. The river is smaller now; much of it on the east is city streets and buildings. The huge lake, Okeechobee, will not flood anymore; it has been ringed by a dike that is forty feet high. The northern Everglades just below the lake has been changed from a lakeshore forest of pond (or custard) apples and moonvine and a river of twelve-foot-high saw grass to fields of sugar cane, growing on the saw-grass peat that accumulated over thousands of years.

Much of the other half of the Glades still has water on it, but the flow is controlled by dikes, gates, and pumping stations. Now the water must serve the voracious appetites of man's urban world as well as the age-old cycles of the nat-

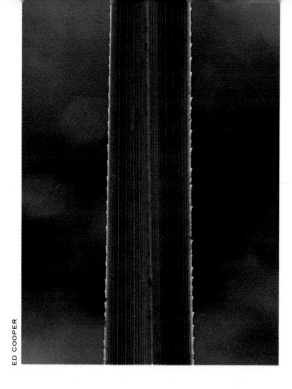

ED COOPER

ural world. South of the Tamiami Trail, however, downstream from the final water-control structures, water flows unimpeded through the Everglades National Park, an area which includes the southern one-seventh of the Everglades.

There are fewer living things now—a few thousand alligators where once there were perhaps a million or more; a few hundred thousand wading birds where once there were several million. Man's works are responsible of course—because the Glades are smaller and the crucial flow of water is controlled—but just exactly what it is that has caused such a dramatic reduction in the numbers of many animal species is a question that biologists are still struggling to answer.

In the meantime, the sun sets over the golden-green saw grass as it always has, and the stillness is broken only by sounds of the nighttime activities of its residents. Day creatures such as the white ibis now flock to their roosts, while black-crowned and yellow-crowned night herons leave their daytime perches and begin to search for crayfish. Limpkins appear, crying their unearthly cry. Fireflies cast faint glows on the backs of the now-active alligators, transformed by the darkness from sluggards to creatures of beauty and swift grace. In the canopied hammocks the blackness is total, and the night-enshrouded world seems to magnify each tiny sound. We are suddenly alive to nature at its fullest and finest— stars, clouds, trees, grasses, breeze, tiny creatures and huge reptiles, water and earth, and an infinite variety of sounds. And in this time of twilight extinguishing into night, we get an exhilarating sense of what this land was like in the dim but not so distant past.

Saw grass is not a grass but a sedge. Sedges are solid and angular in cross-section; as the old saying goes, "Sedges have edges." Saw grass also has "teeth." Even so, deer eat the plant, toothed edges and all.

C. W. PERKINS/ANIMALS ANIMALS

ZIG LESZCZYNSKI/ANIMALS ANIMALS

Amphibians such as the green tree frog abound in the wet world of the Everglades. Tree frogs live not only on trees but on the stems of saw grass and rushes, snatching passing insects for food.

Each animal goes about making its living in its own way. The great egret must feed constantly; the alligator takes a meal once or twice a week.

GLENN VAN NIMWEGEN

THE ISLANDS

Most of the tree-island hammocks are in the southern Everglades. Here hardwoods such as the live oak, mahogany, and gumbo limbo grow in luxuriant profusion on limestone mounds. From the air the hammocks appear as elongated teardrops, the narrow ends pointing downstream. The rotting leaves on the hammock floor mix with rainwater to form an acidic mixture which washes off the island, dissolving the limestone around

Within the quiet, green world of the hammock, eyes must adjust to closely focus on the intimate scene. Out in the saw grass the world seemed infinitely large, and the contrast is abrupt and startling.

and downstream from it. The larger hammocks are therefore surrounded by "moats," and long tails of willows grow in the mud-filled depressions downstream from many.

A walk across the Glades to a hammock is an adventure of the finest kind—though often a wet one—and an exploration of contrasting life communities that can't be excelled anywhere. After the trip through the open saw-grass marsh, the hammock world is dry and "cozy," for the view is now restricted. Most of the larger, older hammocks, however, are open and park-like, once the dense, jungly outer ring of cocoplum or other shrubby growth has been penetrated. The canopy of leaves overhead shades out much of the low-growing shrubbery, and the pigeon plum, palm, and gumbo limbo vie for the sunlight that manages to filter through.

The hammock floor is springy, cushioned by accumulated leaves. Occasionally bedrock can be seen. A solution hole (a spot where the limestone has been eaten down below the water table) provides a distinctly tropical setting, where insects bounce on the water and fish can be spotted that have found their way from the open Glades through underground passages. Besides serving as homes for a variety of life, these solution holes provide humidity for the environment. Together with the surrounding moat, they help protect the tree island from the denuding fires that may now and then sweep through the surrounding Glades.

Each hammock is a world of its own, with different plants and animals. Some are home to the barred owl or red-shouldered hawk. Some

What's out there? A casual look reveals almost nothing, but unseen is the life—some of it large but most of it very small—with which the Everglades teems in its every square inch.

The strangler fig often begins life as an air plant, its seed perhaps dropped on a tree by a bird. As the fig grows, it encircles the tree's trunk, plants itself in the soil and takes over the host tree's place in the hammock canopy.

Liguus tree snails are active only during wet periods. During these times they may descend from the protection of their trees, mate, and lay eggs. Each snail is capable of both fertilizing another snail and laying eggs itself.

CONNIE TOOPS

GLENN VAN NIMWEGEN

contain large live oaks festooned with aerial gardens of ferns, orchids, and strange bromeliads. These "air plants" are not parasites; they are epiphytes which obtain all the moisture and nutrients they need from the air, dew, and dust—using the tree as support without harming it. (Not so the strangler fig, which can eventually crush and fell its host tree.) Tree frogs refresh themselves in the tiny rainwater pools caught and stored by the cupped leaves of bromeliads that look like pineapples—and are in fact members of the pineapple family.

The jewel of the hammock world is the colorful liguus tree-snail, which is often found browsing on the bark of the lysiloma tree and lives only within the hammocks of southern Florida and on the islands of Cuba and Hispaniola. Fifty-eight

varieties of the genus *Liguus*, each with its unique color pattern, occur in the Everglades, but some varieties are present in only one or two hammocks. Their exquisite beauty unfortunately has made them a prime target for collectors, who, by plucking the snails from the hammock trees, decimated their populations and in some cases caused the extinction of certain varieties. Work by park ranger Erwin Winte (after whom one variety has been named) and other conservationists has helped preserve threatened types—rescuing them, for instance, from areas where shopping plazas were being built and transplanting them to hammocks within park boundaries.

The liguus feeds on lichens—combinations of certain algae and fungi which are themselves colorful and unique—scraping them with its rasp-

GLENN VAN NIMWEGEN

Like alligators, turtles need to lounge for long periods in the sun. Besides warming the turtle's reptilian blood, the sun dries and kills back algae and leeches that may be living on the turtle's skin and shell.

Early-morning dews can be both a hindrance and a boon. They ground flying insects until the sun dries their wings enough to fly again, and meanwhile they may fall prey to frogs. But dew nurtures bromeliads and orchids, which collect the water in their gutter-shaped leaves.

ing mouth from the bark of its home tree. The snails are most active during the rainy season and it is then that they descend to the ground to mate and lay eggs. They are able to survive long periods of drought by cementing themselves to the tree bark and *estivating,* a dormancy that lasts until there is again water enough to move about to feed and rebuild their protective seal. Plucking a snail from its estivation spot may therefore cause its death.

Other hammock elements, perhaps less unusual, catch our attention. Amid the tree branches and forests of ferns a quick eye can spot the web of a golden-orb spider, and among the bright leaves on the forest floor perhaps some Indian pottery shards, or even more recent artifacts, may protrude. For it was here, in the hammocks, in which the Indian residents of the Everglades lived and grew their crops. In fact, it is the Indian word *hammocka* ("garden place") which is the source of the term we now use to describe these islands in the Everglades.

And what about snakes? Well, the Everglades of popular mythology, a land teeming with slithering, venomous reptiles, is *partly* true. Snakes are found throughout the Everglades, the hammocks included: Water moccasins may lie in

water just off a hammock; yellow rat-snakes may rest in a tree; the black, shiny indigo may be seen on the hammock floor or in the mangroves. But, of the twenty-six species of snakes found in the park, only *four* carry venom, and that is intended for small prey, not large, two-legged mammals. A careful eye and thoughtful step will avoid any problem with snakes.

Besides the hammock tree-islands, there are other clumps of trees, called *heads,* that grow in the Glades. Some of the heads are leafy mounds often named for their dominant trees. "Bay heads," "coco heads," and "cabbage heads," are dominated by red bay, cocoplum, and cabbage palm, respectively. Like the hammocks, these heads are islands, although not based on a limestone mound like the hardwood hammocks. The leaves dropping from a lone tree build a small mound in which other seeds take root and sprout. Whatever the dominant tree, the resulting head is a dense mass of trees on a low, often soggy, leafy island.

In contrast, bald cypress and willows grow in mud-filled depressions in the bedrock. These are also called heads, and the larger cypress heads are known as *domes.*

Because it has no ears, like all snakes, the corn snake must feel vibrations in the air and ground. Its flicking tongue is actually smelling—gathering scent and delivering it to a gland in the roof of the mouth. Most Everglades snakes are not venomous and are distinguishable from pit vipers by the round pupils in the eye. Please excuse a snake if it seems to stare—it has no eyelids with which to blink!

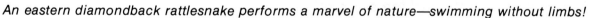

An eastern diamondback rattlesnake performs a marvel of nature—swimming without limbs!

The Piney Rim

At one time, along the eastern rim of the Everglades on the Atlantic Coastal Ridge, a four- to five-mile-wide forest of slash pine existed. (Remnants of this forest can be seen along U.S. 1 and the Florida Turnpike.) Now the only extensive tracts of slash pine left are those which are found in Everglades National Park.

The pinelands on Long Pine Key and other places are rough, rugged, and rocky. The pines seem to grow on nothing at all, their roots uncannily searching and finding the pockets of soil lingering in rock cracks. Years of slow etching and erosion have turned the limestone in the pinelands into sharp spires and jagged holes, making foot travel through the pinelands slow and difficult. The landscape is not only rough, it is also dry, but in the wet season pools of water appear as the water table rises in the limestone. Despite such inhospitable conditions and although the pinelands cover only a small area, they are on the highest and thus the most protected land in southern Florida, so they support over half the plant species found in the park. Among the predominating pines, palms, and palmettos grows a great diversity of shrubs, hardwoods, and occasional bright flowers in a tropical understory accented with temperate plants.

The pineland owes its life to fire. Without fire to keep their numbers under control, the hardwoods growing in the pineland would eventually shade out the pine seedlings and other plants requiring direct sunlight. There are places within the pinelands where this has happened, places which are now hammocks, nearly identical to the hardwood hammocks in the Glades. And while they don't have moats of water surrounding them, as in the Glades, the water standing in solution holes helps prevent the entry of fire into pineland hammocks. Nevertheless, where once there were over five hundred hammocks in the pinelands of Dade County, few remain; these few are located mostly on Long Pine Key and in a few Dade County parks.

Meanwhile, out in the pines, lightning- and man-caused fires may sweep through quickly, burning back the hardwoods and killing them. Not so the slash pine; its multi-layered bark, like a rolled-up newspaper, burns on the outer layers only. Likewise the saw palmetto, companion of pine, often gets burned so much that all its large,

A misty morning in the pinelands softens this rugged country and moistens its dry countenance with welcome dew. Slash pine thrive here, but only with the help of fire, which controls competing trees.

spiky fronds die; but within the tough, thick root the growing heart is protected and within a few weeks has sprouted back.

The saw-grass prairies must also burn periodically to remain healthy. Without fire, saw-grass stands become overgrown with dead, matted saw grass; the young plants cannot survive in the dense growth and the stands die out.

Water and fire, then, are the key elements in the Glades. But since man began to manipulate water, there are times when even a naturally caused fire in the Glades or pinelands is more destructive than beneficial. Dry seasons are often drier than before man came. Solution holes in hammocks go dry more often than in the past, leaving the hammocks more vulnerable to destruction (and some of these hammocks, remember, harbor plant species found nowhere else in the Everglades). However, the National Park Service allows natural fires, under most circumstances, to burn themselves out, since it now considers fire to have a rightful place as a natural force within the Glades. In fact, fire is often "prescribed" in instances where it is deemed necessary to recreate natural historical patterns.

PATRICIA CAULFIELD

The nocturnal opossum swings from a hammock tree.

Long Pine Key—an island of pine, saw palmetto, and hardwood hammocks—is cut by narrow glades of saw grass and grassy marsh. The last remnant of the Everglades pinelands, it is a reminder of the way the land was before Dade County cities sprawled over much of it.

GLENN VAN NIMWEGEN

A wood stork perches mutely amid
cypress and Spanish moss, unaware of the
clouded future he faces because of man's effects
on the Everglades and Big Cypress.

Bald cypress, deprived in winter of
their needles, are cloaked by tapestries of
Spanish moss. Water hyacinth invades
the ancient scene on the ground below.

The Big Cypress Swamp

Not part of the park but contiguous to it and essential to its understanding lies the Big Cypress Swamp. It is a 2,400-square-mile basin to the west of the Glades and separated from the Glades' drainage by a hammock- and cypress-covered ridge. In this basin are deep ponds and long sloughs. These bedrock depressions and the area's acidic soil favor the growth of the bald-cypress tree (locally called just "cypress").

Cypress are found throughout the swamps of

Like gathered monks, cypress knees cluster together.

southeastern United States. Not only can they survive standing for long periods in water, it is in fact necessary to their maintenance, since on dry land other trees would soon crowd them out.

Cousin to the redwood and sequoia of California, the cypress is a deciduous conifer which loses its needles in winter. Like the California giants, it is a large tree, and old. Some of them may have been a century or more old when Columbus arrived in the New World. They make a striking and unforgettable picture—heavy branches draped in ethereal strands of Spanish moss and regal trunks rising from the water like dark columns in some ancient temple.

The bald cypress grows in strands within and along sloughs. Its fascinating, commanding presence is enhanced by an oddity (nature seems at her whimsical best in this country) that is intriguing and puzzling: Curious "knees" that look like tree stumps but actually grow from the roots of the tree stick up through the water and, though their function still eludes botanists, some think that they serve as breathing organs for the tree.

Besides the stands of tall cypress growing in sloughs, there is the smaller pond cypress and its drastically stunted variation, the dwarf cypress, perhaps only three or four feet tall but generally even older than the taller pond cypresses that were more blessed in their choice of soils. Festooned with air plants and ghost orchids, and with bromeliads perched like strange nests in their branches, these trees dot the prairies between the deep sloughs.

Orchids, cypress knees, fluted trunks, and deep, dark pools—these are the things that make up the classic image of a swamp; they are perhaps the source of common misconceptions about the Everglades. But there is more here than cypress and swamp. Prairies of seasonally flooded saw grass, forests of slash pine, hammocks and savannas where there are hardwoods such as willow, oak, pond apple, and red maple provide a landscape that is infinitely varied in the Big Cypress. It is also home to some of the remaining black bear and Florida panther, as well as the more numerous wild turkey and deer.

PATRICIA CAULFIELD

Large bald cypress grow in and along deep water in slow-moving creeks, or sloughs. The alligator flag, like cypress, favors deeper water. For this reason the large-leafed plant served as a clue for alligator hunters earlier in the century.

The last population of panther in the eastern United States is in southern Florida, especially the Big Cypress Swamp Known locally as "Florida panther," the big cat roams over a large territory and is at home in hammock or water. So few panther remain that these animals are now given special legal protection as an "endangered species."

The dwarf cypress, a variety of bald cypress, grows on poorer soil than its larger and often younger relatives. Forests of the little trees occur near Long Pine Key and in the Big Cypress itself.

Perhaps the best place in the Big Cypress Swamp to get a feel for the character of the country is at Corkscrew Swamp Sanctuary, managed by the National Audubon Society, which contains a major remaining stand of bald cypress and the site of a major wood-stork rookery (that is, when the storks have one of their infrequent successful nesting seasons).

The extent of the bald-cypress and associated prairies and hammocks in this part of southern Florida has earned the "big" in Big Cypress; the word is not, as one might suppose, occasioned by the size of the trees. Once, however, there were also some very big trees in those extensive tracts of cypress. But cypress was prized as lumber during the building explosion in the 1940s, and most of the big trees were logged, fortunately excluding the virgin stand at Corkscrew.

GLENN VAN NIMWEGEN

Leafless ghost orchids amid fern

A common bromeliad, wild pine

Cypress trees and dark water is the conception many people still hold of the entire Everglades. Now a portion of this classic swamp world is protected in the Big Cypress National Preserve, adjacent to the park.

Since 1974, when Congress created the Big Cypress National Preserve, about a third of the Big Cypress Swamp has been administered by the National Park Service. In most Park Service areas, the objective is straightforward: to protect the natural features for the enjoyment of people present and future. In a national preserve, however, park managers must not only protect the natural integrity of the land but at the same time monitor certain uses not normally allowed in most national parks: Many private homes already in Big Cypress will remain under private ownership. (In national parks, private land is usually eventually purchased.) In Big Cypress, oil exploration and extraction, cattle grazing, and hunting will continue. And swamp buggies and air boats, not permitted in Everglades National Park, are allowed to operate under some licensing regulations.

It is hoped that in spite of these activities the essential wilderness flavor of the Big Cypress will survive. It has had a close call! Previous to the establishment of the preserve, the Big Cypress and the Everglades itself came perilously close to a monumental invasion of men and machines that would have resulted in irreparable damage to the natural world. In 1968 plans to build a thirty-nine-square-mile jetport on the eastern edge of the swamp, close to Everglades National Park, were nearly complete (indeed, a runway was actually built), and its planners envisioned large cities springing up near the jetport. But a mounting wave of public concern halted the project when it was realized that such a development would seriously and perhaps disastrously damage the quality of Everglades National Park downstream from the jetport site.

The issue also focused attention on the Big Cypress Swamp; it was finally understood that this was an important area to be reckoned with in its own right. Left in its natural state it would provide immeasurable benefit to man for years and years to come, in a way that no sprawling complex of steel and technology ever could.

PATRICIA CAULFIELD

Herons gather where fresh and salt water intermix.

Overleaf: Flamingoes cavort in Florida Bay. They were never common here even when the fishing village near Cape Sable was named for the great birds. The few that wander in nowadays may be escapees from captive flocks or perhaps wild visitors from the Bahamas. Photo by Jim Shives.

THE GREAT ESTUARY

Channeled ever so gently by the Big Cypress Swamp, the Atlantic Coastal Ridge, and several low rock ridges such as the one at Rock Reef Pass, the Everglades drains to the sea in three distinct drainage basins. The fresh water of the Big Cypress Swamp flows southwest into the Ten Thousand Islands, where it meets and mingles with the salt water of the Gulf of Mexico in the dozens of creeks that snake around the maze of mangrove-covered keys.

The central drainage sweeps south out of the heart of the saw-grass glades, bends to the southwest under the influence of Long Pine Key, and surrenders its water to a network of creeks and rivers that in turn meanders to the open Gulf. Shark River, so named for the sharks found in its salty waters, is one of the largest of these rivers. The deeper glades feeding the Shark and other rivers was therefore named "Shark Slough," which flowed through an imperceptible valley—Shark Valley—a basin which lies a few feet lower than the rest of the Glades. In photographs taken from satellites and airplanes, Shark Slough appears as a wide, bending stream of grass dotted with many hammocks.

The third drainage, Taylor Slough, rises north of the main national-park entrance at Chekika State Recreation Area. The slough enters the park, passes through the area of the Anhinga Trail, and proceeds through gaps in the pine-covered ridge to Florida Bay.

Where the fresh water flowing out of the Glades and the Big Cypress Swamp finally meets the sea, yet another change in plant and animal life takes place. Water in this estuary, instead of flowing in a shallow sheet as in the fresh-water Glades, flows in creeks lined first by saw grass and cattail and then by mangroves at it encounters saltier water.

The umbrella-like mangrove, a bizarre, broad-leaved evergreen, is found all through the coastal tropics, and three types exist in the Everglades region—red, black, and white. The trees tolerate or resist salt by excluding it or exuding it from their tissues. The roots of many mangrove forests are submerged in water for much of the year.

The mangroves add to the rich broth of nutrients flowing in from the Glades and the Big Cypress, giving the mangrove estuary a rich diversity of marine life. Pink shrimp, for instance, use it as a nursery and feeding ground, spending their early lives in the mangrove-lined creeks and grow-

Where the Everglades meets the sea, red mangroves push out influences of terrestrial life. Red mangroves are pioneers, creating new land along the coast and keys in Florida Bay and the Gulf of Mexico. These efforts are sometimes arrested by hurricanes, the master sculptors of the tree-fringed coast.

Big Cypress water mingles with sea water as it wanders through the maze of the Ten Thousand Islands.

Black mangroves sprout forests of pneumatophores, strange breathing tubes that encircle the trees in the soft mud. The tree's leaves exude salt on their undersides, an adaptation which helps the black mangrove survive in a harsh environment.

A great white heron takes refuge among the mangroves. This bird is as large as the more common great blue heron and even breeds with it, so that now both birds are considered the same species. (The other large white heron, the great egret, is smaller than the great white and has black instead of yellow legs and feet.) The great white heron was discovered by John James Audubon and is found primarily in Florida Bay and along the Florida Keys.

ing on the plentiful food in the water. As adults they migrate to the open Gulf of Mexico where they provide an important fishery.

The soil in the mangrove estuary, gulf, and bay bottoms is a mixture of limestone, quartz sand, and organic material such as leaves, stems, shells, and other animal remains. To the north in the Ten Thousand Islands, quartz dominates, and many of the islands and creek beds in the area have soils of fine, white sand. Oysters favor this environment, living in extensive oyster beds in tidal areas as well as on red-mangrove roots. Farther to the south, the quartz sand reaches its

limit. Soil nearer to Cape Sable is a limy, pasty-grey mud.

Throughout the coastal region, the mangrove is the predominant terrestrial life form. Its leaves feed a great diversity of aquatic life, but the mangrove region has the least diversity of land plants of any part of the Everglades. In a sense, the region's few plant species have forsaken an easier but more crowded life in the interior for a harder but less competitive life in the brackish, salty water.

It is the red mangrove which is best remembered; its roots arch like crouched "legs"

around its trunk, and a group of mangroves may look like a forest on the march! Such a forest is called a "mangle," and the name is apt. Mangrove roots lie in a thick tangle over soft, leaf-covered, sulfury-smelling mud. Travel in the mangroves is best done by canoe, but a plane is definitely preferable if one is in a hurry!

The mangrove forests act as a coastal barrier —bearing the brunt of waves and storms—and as a land builder, pioneering new land from the sea. Seeds sprout on the parent tree, grow to about a foot in length and then drop off, floating until they lodge on a bit of dry or slightly submerged land. A tree that grows on a shallow bar then begins to drop its leaves, and with the aid of its proplike roots traps sediments and organic debris washed there by the tides. Thus an island or key is born. Some of the larger Florida Bay keys may have been hammocks in fresh-water glades when the level of the sea was lower. Core drilling has brought up samples of saw-grass peat from beneath the mud of Florida Bay, supporting the theory that the oceans are rising.

Behind the red mangroves, farther inland in a zone higher and more sheltered from waves but still washed by salt water, grow the hardy black mangroves. These sprout strange *pneumatophores*,

Rotting mangrove leaves are the key to an abundance and variety of marine life. The leaves and stems serve as food for micro-organisms that in turn support small invertebrates and fish that in turn feed large sport fish such as snook and tarpon.

GLENN VAN NIMWEGEN

37

Everglades wading birds are attracted by exposed fish stranded in mangrove creeks by the falling tide. Tidal fluctuations and seasonal drying in the inland fresh-water marshes make available a wealth of food for these birds.

or breathing tubes, that look like forests of short soda-straws surrounding the trunk. Still farther inland stand the white mangroves and buttonwoods, which favor drier, higher land. They form hammocks that may also include gumbo limbo and mahogany.

All the plants of these salty regions have specialized leaves. Some plants on the coastal prairies and near Cape Sable beaches grow succulent, fleshy leaves; pickleweed and glasswort are tasty examples. Unless a plant has a mechanism to remove salt from the water it draws, it must depend on rainfall for all of its fresh water. And since rainfall is seasonal and the salty soils of the

Fiddler crabs gather in an open-air convention.

coastal prairies and mangroves can draw water out of plants, these dry areas support desert plants—yucca, and cacti such as the prickly pear!

The mangrove is the key to the variety and abundance of aquatic life in the Everglades estuary. The tough leaves rarely succumb to parasites or other infections. But when a mangrove sheds a leaf into the water, its energy begins to become a part of the food chain. Bacteria and fungi attack the newly fallen leaf, which with stems and other debris from the trees makes up *detritus*. It may take as long as six months for microorganisms to begin the breakdown of a mangrove leaf. Once it does begin to disintegrate, to become detritus, the leaf becomes food for other microscopic animals such as various protozoa. A bit of mangrove detritus has more food value than the original leaf or stem—it is now enriched by the bacteria, fungi, and algae that attacked it. Nematodes and protozoa that eat bits of mangrove detritus then fall prey to shrimp and small fish, who in turn are food for larger game fish—including snapper, mullet, red drum, and tarpon, as well as blue crab, stone crab, and spiny lobster.

Besides being vital to a healthy fishery, mangroves provide a bulwork against the hurricanes and their storm surges that often hit the coast with ferocious intensity and can raise the tide level by as much as twenty feet. The next hurricane to hit the Florida Keys and other areas where mangroves have been removed recently

Low-growing, spider-like red mangroves signal the transition at the edge where fresh and salt waters meet. The high water of autumn is fresh, but by spring the water that remains is brackish.

Glasswort, sea purslane, and pickleweed grow on the Cape Sable coastal prairie. These plants live in a desert-like environment where salty soil and hot sun easily desiccate plants less adaptable.

Cape Sable beaches are not sandy but shelly! Fragments of bay and sea shells are pounded, ground, and deposited by waves in long, arcing, sparkling-white beaches.

Wood stork, or "ironhead"

may well reveal the importance of the role mangroves play in this defensive capacity.

Mangroves and other trees on the mainland of southern Florida and on the small Florida Bay keys provide roosting and nesting space for much of the spectacular bird life of the Everglades. Because in various seasons they harbor nesting birds—bald eagles, ospreys, roseate spoonbills, wood storks, great white herons, reddish egrets, great egrets, snowy egrets, and the several other herons—all but a few of the Florida Bay keys have been closed to human landings.

From the rookeries, wading birds range far and wide—into the Glades drying in the winter, to mud flats in the Gulf, to bay waters during the falling tide to capture shellfish and small fish, to creeks in the mangrove forest, and to ponds in the Big Cypress. Wood storks (the only stork in North America) may, for instance, fly seventy-five miles from rookery to feeding ground. Until recently, birds traditionally followed the drying patterns in the Glades: In December, usually, wood storks fed in the mangrove zone. By January and February, storks moved into the southern Shark Slough and still later into pools left along the edge of the slough and others scattered throughout the Glades.

The American crocodile makes its last stand in Everglades National Park. The crocodile can be distinguished from the blunt-nosed, black-backed alligator by its long, narrow snout and olive-green color. The Everglades is the one place in the world where both alligators and crocodiles are found. Alligators live in the fresh-water marshes and crocodiles live in salty and brackish waters. Crocodiles now number only a few hundred, and only a dozen active nests have been identified.

River otter are most easily found in the spring season, when drought concentrates them near remaining water and their food, crayfish.

STOUFFER PRODUCTIONS/ANIMALS ANIMALS

The wood stork, a prodigious eater, feeds not by sighting its prey, but by feeling for fish with its sensitive bill; when the bill encounters a fish, it snaps shut instantly and reflexively. The young of the wood stork take four or five months to fledge, and their appetites are just as keen as their parents. The adult wood storks must literally "bump" into tons of fish! Thus the nesting success of the wood stork depends upon the health of fish populations and the density in which fish concentrate in the dry season, factors which in turn are affected by disturbances in the flow and extent of fresh water in the Glades. This is why the wood stork is often considered a "barometer" of the health of the Everglades as a whole.

Since 1962, when flood gates installed under the Tamiami Trail controlled the flow of water into the southern Everglades, wood storks—during all but a few nesting seasons—have either failed to nest at all or have abandoned their nests. The cause is probably lack of food, but Park Service and Audubon Society biologists continue to search for the exact cause of nesting failure and the means to correct the problem. Meanwhile the feathered spectacle of pink and white and blue continues to dwindle.

The tangled roots of a mangrove sentinel curtain a view of shallow Florida Bay, now calm as the dawn.

ED COOPER

The Feathered

White ibis, the ''Chokoloskee chicken''

Laughing gull in summer plumage

JAMES A. KERN

R. F. HEAD/ANIMALS ANIMALS

Spectacle

The feathered spectacle of the Everglades has attracted people for over a hundred years. Early on, Audubon himself came to capture and record the beauty of these birds with paint and canvas. Later others came hunting for the then fashionable and highly prized feathers themselves, decimating bird populations alarmingly. Today people come to admire and wonder, to photograph, or to record the remarkable sights upon their memories. The feathered spectacle is not a year-round phenomenon. It occurs only during the dry season, when fresh water evaporates from the Glades and that important food—fish—is concentrated and easily caught by these most glamorous of all birds.

Roseate spoonbill in full breeding colors

CHARLES MAGNAGHI

GLENN VAN NIMWEGEN

Back in 1870, when only 85 people lived along the coast of southeastern Florida, an estimated 2 million wading birds (herons, egrets, storks, and spoonbills) inhabited the Everglades during dry seasons. During the late 19th century, plume hunting reduced these birds to only several hundred thousand. This dramatic loss spurred protective laws in Florida--and in New York, where the plumes had been shipped to millinery houses. Thus protected, the wading-bird population rebounded to near its original level. Then, in the 1940s and after, the character of the Everglades itself began to change. As South Florida grew, the Everglades shrank, its waters controlled for man's uses. By the mid-1970s, wading-bird numbers had dropped back to a few hundred thousand--about ten percent of what it had been a century before. Biologists actively study these birds, looking for clues that might lead to stopping or even reversing the decline. As yet the only thing that is certain is that life in the Everglades is more fragile than anyone ever thought.

An adult brown pelican.

A preening great egret.

GLENN VAN NIMWEGEN

Other herons might stand quietly waiting for a chance to strike at a passing fish. Not so the snowy egret; this bird is a restless, active feeder. The process involves first keeping a proper distance from other feeding birds. Then, skimming over open water, the snowy begins herding fish, which flee before its outspread wings and golden feet dragging through the water. Soon the snowy snatches its prey and eats it in flight. It's all over in a matter of moments.

Numbering only several hundred in Florida, the snail kite is a rare sight. This hawk-like bird feeds exclusively on the fresh-water apple snail and is most numerous in the area north of Everglades National Park.

SEQUENCE BY JAMES A. KERN

Limpkin, the "night crier"

CONNIE TOOPS

PAT TOOPS

Some Everglades birds, such as this yellow-crowned night heron, leave the roost only at night. The calls of night herons, owls, limpkins, pig frogs, and other night creatures create a special world experienced only after sunset.

PATRICIA CAULFIELD

Family portrait: black-necked stilts

DOLLY MAGNAGHI

An immature little blue heron, before molting blue

Male anhinga, displaying breeding plumage

GLENN VAN NIMWEGEN

PATRICIA CAULFIEL

Tricolored (Louisiana) heron, Audubon's favorite

A flashy beauty, the purple gallinule

The heron family members have long legs and necks and straight bills. Unlike cranes and storks, herons fly with the necks folded into an "S." They are primarily fish eaters, although great blue herons occasionally take baby alligators and cattle egrets eat insects. Each heron has a color scheme uniquely its own, for plumage, legs, feet, and bill. If one pays very close attention to a heron's foot, one would see a little comb on the middle toenail!

GLENN VAN NIMWEGEN

A bald eagle screams from his roost in Florida Bay

Roseate spoonbills wade near the mangroves

LYNN STONE/ANIMALS ANIMALS

Double-crested cormorant, a diving sea bird

Angel wings illumine the snowy egret

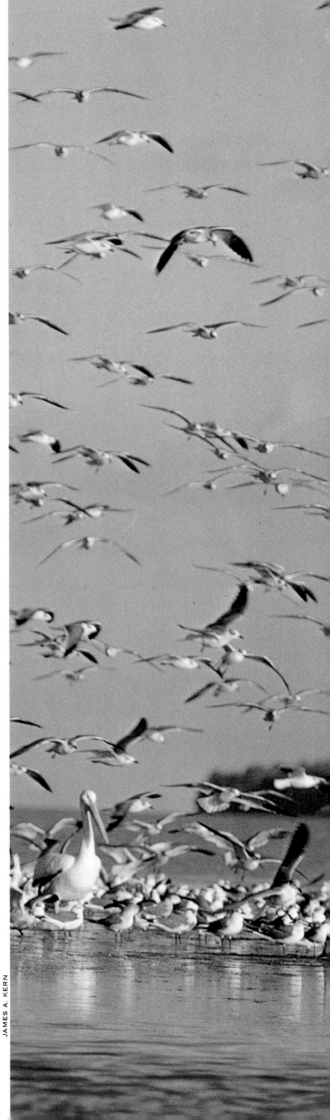

Brazilian pepper

GLENN VAN NIMWEGEN

THE THREAT OF EXOTICS

The peninsula's warm, moist climate makes it an ideal place for living things—from the fungus that causes mildew in the closets of South Florida residences to the primitive monarch of the Glades, the alligator. And so the region has become a home for plants and animals not native to Florida. Many of the plants growing in Miami and other South Florida cities were imported for ornamental uses. And once they find their way into the Everglades, whether by plan or accident, many of these exotic plants and animals undergo population explosions—set in motion by the lack of local natural checks on their numbers such as were present in their original homes. A few walking catfish, imported from South America and casually dumped into a Florida pond in the 1960s, multiplied and literally "walked" from one body of water to another until today their progeny of thousands all across Florida compete for food and space with native fish.

The destructive effect of exotic plants on native associations of plants is felt in turn by native animal life. The Australian pine, which lines farm fields near Homestead and some highways in southern Florida, is an aggressive invader. It thrives on disturbed soil, particularly that left in the wake of hurricanes, where native trees have been uprooted. Once established, Australian pines exclude all other plants by covering the ground with their stems and branches and shading out all comers. In some coastal areas Australian pine has taken over sandy beaches that until then had been nest sites for sea turtles and the American crocodile, already rare.

Other exotic invaders include *maleluca*, or *cajeput*, an Australian tree that invades disturbed or burned areas and replaces all native vegetation, and whose offensive secretions drive away the animal life. Brazilian pepper is particularly abundant in the Hole-in-the-Donut, a recently purchased area inside the park that until 1975 had been intensively farmed.

Water hyacinth, brought to Florida because of its beautiful flower, nevertheless clogs waterways, disrupts native food chains by shading out bottom-dwelling plants, and thus affects native fish populations. Millions of dollars are spent each year to control the water hyacinth in Florida's rivers and canals and in some of the waters of Everglades National Park.

Life in the Everglades is in delicate balance, a balance that man, not nature, now controls. During the last century he has altered key elements of that balance. With dynamite, bullets, and steel, he has diverted rivers, slaughtered wildlife, and felled forests. But man has lately become a wiser animal. He now realizes that if he is to control the water he must likewise manage fire to maintain native plant and animal communities. He now knows that the plants and animals he has introduced sometimes challenge and destroy the natural order that took millions of years to evolve.

And so, he has learned that he must protect the unique flora and fauna in the Everglades. Every park in America is precious, but Everglades National Park is a treasure unmatched anywhere. It is a treasure that could, without constant care and vigilant guardianship, disappear under our very noses.

SUGGESTED READING

Cox, W. Eugene. *in pictures Everglades: The Continuing Story.* Las Vegas, NV: KC Publications, Inc., 1989.

Davidson, Treat. "Tree Snails, Gems of the Everglades." *National Geographic*, March, 1965.

Fleming, Glenn; Pierre Genelle; and Robert W. Long, *Wild Flowers of Florida.* Miami: Banyan Books, Inc., 1976.

George, Jean Craighead. *Everglades Wildguide.* Washington, D.C.: U.S. Government Printing Office, 1972.

Gore, Rick. "Florida, Noah's Ark for Exotic Newcomers." *National Geographic*, October, 1976.

Gore, Rick. "Twilight Hope for Big Cypress." *National Geographic*, August, 1976.

Water hyacinth

Those Who Came Before . . .

Prior to the twentieth century, the Everglades was only lightly touched by the presence of man. From the time of the arrival of the first Indians about two thousand years ago to the founding of Miami in 1896, people either lived in small, tenuous settlements or simply passed by the area, stopping for game, seafood, or water. It is only in the twentieth century that man's effect on the natural ecosystems of southern Florida has been so dramatic.

When the Spaniards arrived in the early 1500s, they found the descendants of the early Indians living along both coasts of Florida. Over a period of time, these groups had lived in separation and had differentiated into two related tribes: the *Tequesta*, who lived on the east coast

ZIG LESZCZYNSKI/ANIMALS ANIMALS

Canoeists can travel from Everglades City to Flamingo along a hundred-mile, marked route through narrow mangrove-lined creeks and across open bays. Such a trip provides time for leisurely savoring the Everglades, a necessity in order to enjoy it fully.

JAMES A. KERN

Cypress trunks, laboriously burned and chopped, make excellent dugout canoes. Prior to the drainage efforts of the white men, Indians used canoes for as much as ten months out of the year. Miccosukees and Seminoles even traveled across the Glades in outriggered sail canoes!

from what is now Pompano Beach into the Florida Keys, and the *Calusa,* who lived along the southwestern coast, especially around the Caloosahatchee River. Evidence of the presence of both the Tequesta and the Calusa has been found on Cape Sable, although the Calusa apparently were dominant there.

The mounds left behind by the Tequesta and especially the Calusa have yielded valuable information about them and their ways of life. Because of the natural bounty of southern Florida, these Indians were able to live in permanent villages in their houses of mud and shell while pursuing a hunting-and-gathering economy.

Shellfish, sea turtles, fish, inland game animals, and wild plants—all of which were available the year around—made up their diet, suggesting that they were fishermen who went to sea. (An account by the Spaniard Hernando d'Escalante Fontaneda who, having been shipwrecked at the age of thirteen off the southeastern coast of Florida, lived with the Tequesta from 1545 to 1562, reveals that they also ate "sea wolf," the possibly extinct West Indian seal.) Coontie, a palmlike plant found throughout the pineland that yields an edible, starchy root, was also part of their diet, as it was for the later Seminoles and white settlers.

Miccosukee and Seminole Indians once traded game for colorful cloth and sewing machines, which they still favor and use with skill. The cabbage palm continues to provide thatching for their houses, chickees, *which take advantage of the breezes for natural air conditioning.*

The tools of the Tequesta and Calusa included conch-shell hammers, shark-tooth knives, and pots made from the marl soil of the Everglades. While most of the Indians probably lived outside the area that is now Everglades National Park, some important shell mounds exist in or near the park today. Chokoloskee, near Everglades City, is itself built on a gigantic mound that covers 135 acres and is twenty feet high in places! And an ancient canal was built close to the site of the present-day Bear Lake Canal near Flamingo.

In the early 1500s, when Ponce de Leon and the Spaniards arrived in southern Florida in search of youth and gold, there were approximately eight hundred Tequesta and two thousand Calusa. Both tribes successfully resisted attempts to subjugate them, and the Spanish missions failed. The Spanish presence in southern Florida was therefore never significant in terms of impact on its inhabitants.

Spain gave Florida to Britain in 1763, and when the Spaniards left, the Tequesta and Calusa suddenly seem to have vanished from the Florida scene. Some of the Indians may have left with the Spaniards for islands in the Caribbean, and some may have been killed or captured in raids by the incoming Creek Indians, but most of them had probably succumbed to the diseases brought by the Europeans.

After 1700, certain members of the Creek Confederation, a loosely knit group of Indians in Alabama and Georgia, began moving into Florida to escape pressures from expanding English colonies to the north. Initially, these Hichiti-speaking peoples, the Miccosukees, settled in northern Florida. They were followed by another branch of the Creeks, the Muskogees, a migration that occurred around 1814 after the Creek's war with U.S. forces led by Andrew Jackson.

By 1821, when Florida had been formally ceded to the United States by Spain (having been given back by the British in 1784), the two groups of immigrant Creeks in Florida numbered 5,000 people and were collectively known as the Seminoles. They lived in northern Florida, but occasionally in the 1820s their hunting parties did venture into southern Florida. The knowledge of the country thus gained would soon prove invaluable to them.

Meanwhile, the clashes between the Seminoles and the settlers, which had been going on for years, continued to grow hotter (partly because the Seminoles had long provided sanctuary for runaway slaves), and raids on the Indians became harsher. Finally, forced into a reservation in central Florida where they were promised much and instead suffered miserably, the angry Seminoles retaliated, raiding white settlements. The settlers demanded their immediate removal.

Thus in 1830, the United States, under Andrew Jackson, who was now the President, began its now-infamous policy of Indian removal, which meant that Indians living east of the Mississippi River were to be moved to the west of it. There lay what Americans at the time called the "Great American Desert," thought to be a useless, barren land where white civilization would never go—and therefore a good place to send Indians! This solution was seen as a way to prevent further hostilities between the Indians and whites and at the same time acquire coveted Indian lands.

Many tribes went peaceably down the "Trail of Tears" to Indian Territory, in present-day Oklahoma; some Seminole bands, however, led by the proud and rebellious Osceola, resisted with legendary success. But the odds eventually proved too great, and thousands, too weak to resist any more, were finally shipped west. Others, weakened also but too proud to give up, retreated farther and farther south, finally finding refuge in the Everglades and especially the Big Cypress.

The Army pursued the Seminoles, but unlike their quarries, led by the militant Chekika, they were hampered by a complete ignorance of southern Florida's interior. They had the maps made by the Spaniards, but they were based only on conjecture and the reports of the Calusa. Some of these maps showed a huge lake running the length of southern Florida; others showed a lake, *La Gran Laguna de Mayaimi* (the Army came to know the lake by its Seminole name, Okeechobee), and a vague, vast marsh to the south. It could be said that these elusive Seminoles were responsible for the white man's first expedition across the Everglades!

Gradually the war against the Seminoles petered out, but not without having taken an expensive toll. (It had cost the government $20 million, years and years of fighting, and the lives of 1,500 soldiers!) In the end, only about 150 fugitives were left. These people lived, forgotten now, in their villages of picturesque, thatched-roofed *chickees*, huts supported by cypress poles and open to the breezes. They raised crops—corn, squash, oranges, and cane—and traded animal skins for money with which they bought cloth and metal products such as guns, knives, pots and pans—and sewing machines, with which they fashioned the colorful garments for which they have since become famous.

The Seminoles' secluded way of life ended with the completion of the Tamiami Trail (linking Tampa and Miami) in 1928. With this first road across the Everglades and Big Cypress came the white hunters, oilmen, and others. Today the Muskogee-speakers live in several Seminole Indian reservations near Alligator Alley, and the Miccosukees—the Hichiti-speakers—live in a series of villages along the Tamiami Trail. Their primary business is now tourism, but they remain an independent people, proud and protective of their unique culture and history.

After the Seminole Wars, the Everglades was

JAMES A. KERN

Airboats in the wet season and swamp buggies in the dry season are uniquely Everglades' conveyances. No private airboats or buggies operate in the park; only those manned by rangers on patrol and researchers on assignment travel the park's back country on established trails. Uncontrolled airboat or buggy use scars the landscape; outside the park, the land is criss-crossed with tracks.

The long feathers of the snowy egret, aigrettes, were prized for decorating ladies' hats at the turn of the century. These plumes are grown only during nesting season, so when the adult birds were shot, their young—left exposed in the nest—died too.

DOLLY MAGNAGHI

forgotten. Florida itself was passed by in the rush to settle the western frontier, and it was not until 1845 that this last southeastern state was admitted to the Union. As late as 1870, for example, Dade County—which then also included present-day Broward and Palm Beach counties—had a population of eighty-five souls. (The same three counties now include over three million people, about a third of Florida's population!

Interest in the Everglades and southern Florida revived in the 1880s, when the New Orleans' *Times-Democrat* carried enticing reports of two expeditions it had sponsored: The first had viewed the initial drainage efforts around the Kissimmee River, Lake Okeechobee's major tributary; and the second had explored the Caloosahatchee River to Okeechobee and then through the Glades to Shark River.

Such vivid journalism did bring settlers during the latter part of the nineteenth century, and these people made their living in southern Florida by fishing and by salvaging the many ships that either ran aground on the coral reefs on the eastern coast or were rendered helpless by hur-

ricanes. Some made a living by shooting plume birds and shipping the coveted breeding plumes to the New York millinery industry. Plumes of herons and the snowy and great egrets were preferred. These beautiful birds were usually shot while on the nest, so that the unattended young died as well as the adult birds. Plume-bird populations declined at an alarming rate.

Charles W. Pierce described one of these plume-hunting trips in 1886. His account is remarkable for its documenting of the indiscriminant shooting of hundreds of birds of all kinds. It is also remarkable because it tells of a *sailing* journey, in the month of *April*, up the Miami River, past the Miami Falls (now under the 27th-Avenue interchange), into the Everglades. Less than a hundred years later, April—the height of the dry season—is a time for walking, not sailing, in the Everglades!

Most of the few small settlements scattered around the coastal region were fishing villages, such as Chokoloskee and Flamingo. Others were centers for processing local raw materials, such as bark for tanin. Miami, meanwhile, was experi-

The Everglades has no flowering season. Flowers bloom throughout the year, each in its own season. The pinelands nurture most of the flowering plants, but hammocks, glades, and coastal prairie all contribute their special varieties.

Horned bladderwort

GLENN VAN NIMWEGEN

Buttonbush

PATRICIA CAULFIELD

JIM SHIVES

Glades lobelia

encing a sudden burst of growth, spurred by Henry Flagler's railroad, which had in 1896 reached Miami. Hugh Willoughby, who was one of the last to adventure into the untamed Everglades, in 1897 poled his canoe from Shark River across the open Glades to the Miami River, passed the falls, and neared Miami. And here he received quite a shock, for during the months that he had been away the sleepy supply post had become a thriving city of many buildings and several streets—in Willoughby's view, a change that was a bit much and a bit too fast!

In the early years of the twentieth century, Florida's governor, Napoleon Bonaparte Broward, activated an idea that had tantalized generations of Floridians. The theory was that, since water runs downhill, a few canals could be dug, the water drained off the Everglades, and *voila!*—land for cities and farms. So in 1909, the state's Everglades Drainage District completed the Miami Canal connecting Lake Okeechobee to the Miami River and the sea. Other canals followed.

Some land south of Lake Okeechobee did become available for farming. But two hurricanes,

one in 1926 and the other in 1928, swept Okeechobee over the low dike that had been built around it, and thousands died in the resulting floods. The tragedies led to the involvement of the federal government, and in 1930 the Army Corps of Engineers built the Hoover Dike around the lake.

Drainage and canal-building went on, but the dream of new land became instead a nightmare of problems. Without its usual protective layer of water, the organic soil of the Everglades oxidized away. Fires burned out of control, smoldering in the organic peat now parched by drought. Salt water entered the Biscayne Aquifer, fouling water wells in Miami. Finally the ecological significance of the Everglades and its effect on all of South Florida began to dawn on its citizens!

A hurricane in 1947 that brought flood waters right up into the streets of Dade County was the catalyst which stirred action to impose order on the water-management chaos, and 1949 saw the establishment of the Central and Southern Florida Flood Control District. The district and its successor, the South Florida Water Management District, set about to prevent flooding during the rainy season and prevent destruction of the Everglades during drought. And it sought to maintain the fresh-water pressure head on the Biscayne Aquifer to prevent salt water from getting into that water-holding rock formation.

The year 1947 was a landmark year. Not only did it bring that great hurricane, it also marked an event in which the preservation of the Everglades for its own sake became a recognized factor in the South Florida equation. That was the year that Everglades National Park was established, dedicated by President Harry S. Truman in Everglades City.

The park's creation was the culmination of many efforts over many years. The Audubon Society began protective measures in the early part of the century by posting wardens at plume-bird rookeries. Just how ruthless the plume hunters had become was demonstrated by the 1905 murder of one of the society's wardens, Guy Bradley, at his Everglades post.

Other efforts followed. In 1916 the Florida Federation of Women's Clubs helped establish and maintain the Royal Palm State Park, protecting Paradise Key on the edge of Taylor Slough. In 1929, the state of Florida created the Tropical Everglades National Park Commission, headed by Ernest F. Coe. The commission was not entirely successful; it was given a purpose—to acquire land—but no money with which to do it.

Then in 1934 the U.S. Congress passed a bill authorizing a park in the Everglades. The maximum boundaries envisioned for this park would have included much of the Big Cypress Swamp and Key Largo, including the coral reef now within John D. Pennekamp Coral Reef State Park. But still no funds were authorized with which to purchase land. Eventually, efforts by Coe and Pennekamp (of the *Miami Herald*) paid off. Spurred by the state government's post-World War II allocation of land and $2 million for the purchase of privately owned land within park boundaries, many people came forward to donate land, including Barron G. Collier, who owned most of Collier County. So at last the park was a reality.

But its creation was only a beginning in the struggle to preserve the Everglades and its wildlife. Continued development in South Florida, and water management practices designed to provide water supply and flood control for urban and agricultural areas, have reduced the amount

Prickly-pear cactus

Clamshell orchid

JIM SHIVES

Since the Everglades offers no extensive fields of colorful bloom nor mountain backdrop, it may take more time and care to appreciate than parks which have such displays. The Everglades is a vast area and its charms are in its infinitesimal detail. Each tiny part is a wondrous experience, and each Everglades' encounter—such as happening upon one of its delicate, solitary blossoms—is a delight that asks for more and then more.

Orchid collecting, like tree-snail collecting, threatened to obliterate certain forms from the Everglades. The collecting of orchids (or any natural feature for that matter) is prohibited in the park; thus they are protected for the pleasure of all Everglades' visitors.

Swamp lily

Morning glory

Taylor Slough is the smallest but most visited of the drainages in the Everglades. It is crossed by the Anhinga Trail, where man-made borrow pits make in effect a large gator hole. Here wildlife can be viewed at close range, as in a zoo. But unlike a zoo, there are no cages and for the animals scant protection from the environmental adversities caused by mankind.

GLENN VAN NIMWEGEN

of fresh water going into the Everglades.

The extent of the Everglades ecosystem is so vast and intricate that no single group or agency can begin to address its restoration. There are no quick fixes for the Everglades. Restoration of water flows, and buffer lands to protect private interests adjacent to wetlands, will require a coordinated, cooperative effort to achieve any measure of success.

SUGGESTED READING

CARTER, LUTHER J. *The Florida Experience*. Baltimore: The Johns Hopkins Univ. Press, 1974.

DAVIS, STEVEN M. AND JOHN C. OGDEN. *Everglades: The Ecosystem and Its Restoration*. Delray Beach, FL: St. Lucie Press, 1994.

TEBEAU, CHARLTON W. *History of Florida*. Coral Gables: Univ. of Miami Press, 1971.

TEBEAU, CHARLTON W. *Man in the Everglades*. Coral Gables: Univ. of Miami Press, 1976.

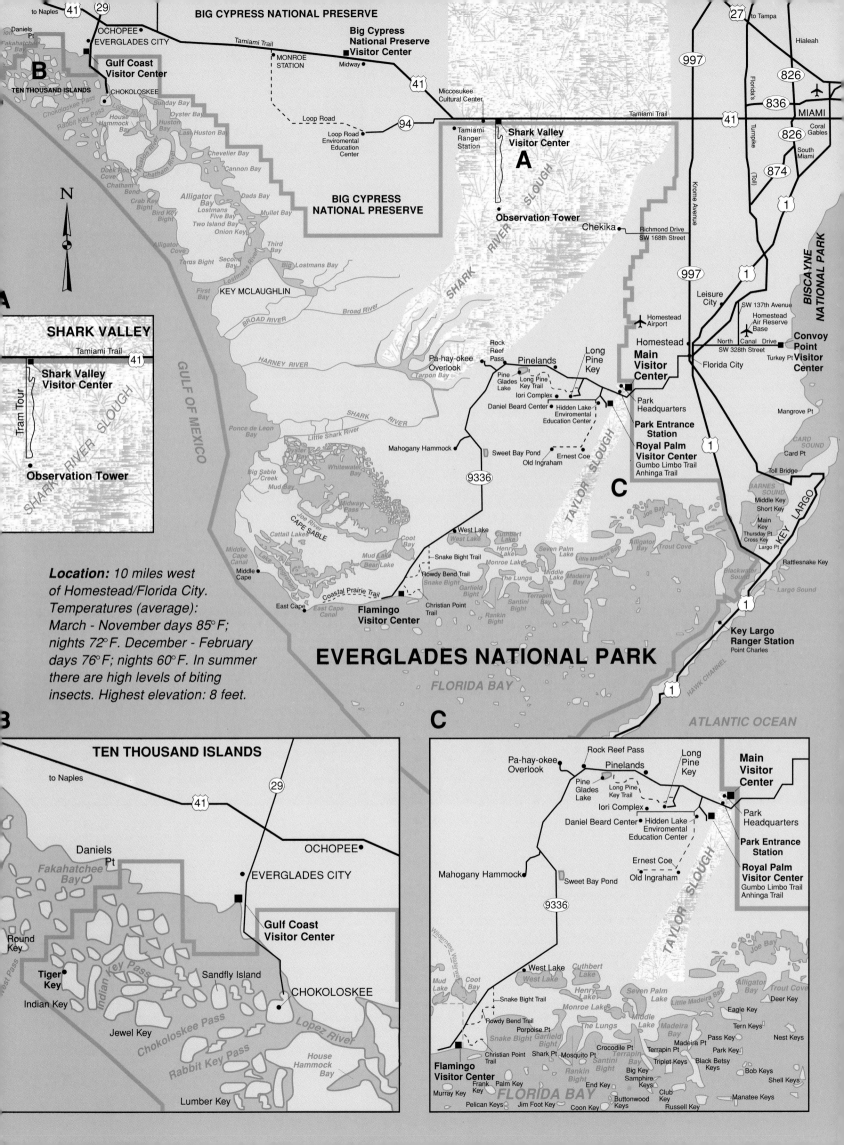

The result of all these efforts is an astonishing anachronism. Next to one of America's largest and busiest cities lies one of America's largest concentrations of national-park land outside Alaska. Here the life—which is after all the quintessential nature of the Everglades—finds a beleaguered refuge. Here man tries to compensate for his headlong rush to a future of mechanized complexity by slowing time and paying homage to an irreplaceable wildness—here, in the Everglades, an original but penetrable wilderness that can yet speak to us of an age primeval and profound.

TOM TILL

Sunsets are spectacular in the Everglades as here at Paurotis Pond.

Books on National Park areas in "The Story Behind the Scenery" series are: Acadia, Alcatraz Island, Arches, Badlands, Big Bend, Biscayne, Blue Ridge Parkway, Bryce Canyon, Canyon de Chelly, Canyonlands, Cape Cod, Capitol Reef, Channel Islands, Civil War Parks, Colonial, Crater Lake, Death Valley, Denali, Devils Tower, Dinosaur, Everglades, Fort Clatsop, Gettysburg, Glacier, Glen Canyon-Lake Powell, Grand Canyon, Grand Canyon-North Rim, Grand Teton, Great Basin, Great Smoky Mountains, Haleakalā, Hawai`i Volcanoes, Independence, Joshua Tree, Lake Mead-Hoover Dam, Lassen Volcanic, Lincoln Parks, Mammoth Cave, Mesa Verde, Mount Rainier, Mount Rushmore, Mount St. Helens, National Park Service, National Seashores, North Cascades, Olympic, Petrified Forest, Redwood, Rocky Mountain, Scotty's Castle, Sequoia & Kings Canyon, Shenandoah, Statue of Liberty, Theodore Roosevelt, Virgin Islands, Yellowstone, Yosemite, Zion.

Additional books in "The Story Behind the Scenery" series are: Annapolis, Big Sur, California Gold Country, California Trail, Colorado Plateau, Columbia River Gorge, Fire: A Force of Nature, Grand Circle Adventure, John Wesley Powell, Kauai, Lake Tahoe, Las Vegas, Lewis & Clark, Monument Valley, Mormon Temple Square, Mormon Trail, Mount St. Helens, Nevada's Red Rock Canyon, Nevada's Valley of Fire, Oregon Trail, Oregon Trail Center, Santa Catalina, Santa Fe Trail, Sharks, Sonoran Desert, U.S. Virgin Islands, Water: A Gift of Nature, Whales.

Call (800-626-9673), fax (702-433-3420), or write to the address below.

Published by KC Publications, 3245 E. Patrick Ln., Suite A, Las Vegas, NV 89120.

Tomorrow's hope, now an awkward young, great blue heron; photo by Lynn M. Stone/Animals Animals

Back cover: Ibis rest unmolested in the foliage at Corkscrew Sanctuary; photo by David Muench.

Created, Designed, and Published in the U.S.A.
Printed by Doosan Dong-A Co., Ltd., Seoul, Korea
Color Separations by Kedia/Kwang Yang Sa Co., Ltd.
Paper produced exclusively by Hankuk Paper Mfg. Co., Ltd.